Published in Great Britain in MMXX by
Book House, an imprint of
The Salariya Book Company Ltd
25 Marlborough Place, Brighton BN1 1UB
www.salariya.com

ISBN: 978-1-912904-20-4

© The Salariya Book Company Ltd MMXX

All rights reserved. No part of this publication may be reproduced, stored in or introduced into a retrieval system or transmitted in any form, or by any means (electronic, mechanical, photocopying, recording or otherwise) without the written permission of the publisher. Any person who does any unauthorised act in relation to this publication may be liable to criminal prosecution and civil claims for damages.

1 3 5 7 9 8 6 4 2

A CIP catalogue record for this book is available from the British Library.

Printed and bound in Turkey.

This book is sold subject to the conditions that it shall not, by way of trade or otherwise, be lent, resold, hired out, or otherwise circulated without the publisher's prior consent in any form or binding or cover other than that in which it is published and without similar condition being imposed on the subsequent purchaser.

Author: Roger Canavan
Illustrator: Damian Zain
Editor: Nick Pierce

Visit
www.salariya.com
for our online catalogue and
free fun stuff.

This book was researched using the resources available on the Plimoth Plantation website: www.plimoth.org

ADVENTURES IN THE REAL WORLD
1620 VOYAGE OF THE MAYFLOWER

WRITTEN BY
ROGER CANAVAN

ILLUSTRATED BY
DAMIAN ZAIN

BOOK HOUSE
a SALARIYA imprint

• 1620 VOYAGE OF THE MAYFLOWER •

INTRODUCTION

Norman, a sleek, tubby rat, sits comfortably on a pile of boxes in a cluttered cellar. Light streams through cracks between the floorboards above him. The sound of human voices and the occasional burp can be heard as a human family works its way through a feast up above.

Fletch, Norman's young nephew, scrambles up the boxes to get a better look through the cracks between the floorboards. He can see the room above and calls down to his uncle:

• ADVENTURES IN THE REAL WORLD •

'Mmmm, Thanksgiving: my most favourite day of the year! All those scrumptious crumbs and bits of food slipping down through the floorboards to our cellar. Oooh! What's that? Something just plopped on the cellar floor? Cranberry sauce?'

'Yes, looks like it. I bet you didn't know that the Pilgrims had never heard of cranberry sauce – or cranberries – when they arrived here in Massachusetts?'

'The who?' A dollop of sauce dribbles from Fletch's mouth.

'You know, the Pilgrims. The people who sailed across from England to start new lives over here. They all called it "the New World".'

'Was that last month? I saw a big yacht with a British flag out in Plymouth harbour.'

'Last month? No! You cannot be serious. It was about four hundred years ago. And the Plymouth that you and I know

• 1620 VOYAGE OF THE MAYFLOWER •

here - and where you saw that yacht - was named after Plymouth in England, where they sailed from.'

Norman sighed. He could see that he'd have a lot of explaining to do. 'If they hadn't set sail, then you and I wouldn't be tucking into turkey and sweet potatoes, pumpkin pie or cranberry sauce. Like other English rats, we'd have to get by on lardy cake and bubble-and-squeak. And something weird called Marmite, which looks like tar and tastes like salty.... ugh, don't get me started on that.'

'Hmm. So these humans - these Pilgrims - left everything behind in order to settle here and meet the local folk in America?'

'Well, you're right about leaving everything behind, or almost everything', Norman explained. 'As for wanting to meet the local people, the Wampanoag nation, that's a little different. A bit trickier. The real reason had more to do with what they were leaving behind in England than what - or who - they

• ADVENTURES IN THE REAL WORLD •

expected to find over here. I doubt if they had given much thought to the people who already lived here.'

'But at least they thought ahead and remembered to pack lots of rats on their ship. What was the ship called?' Fletch was interested, but was keeping an eye out for any more morsels of food from above.

'The *Mayflower*. And you're right. Rats did make the trip over along with those Pilgrims. But they were mainly stowaways, along for the ride. Humans are afraid of us, as you probably know. And those rats that made the first trip across the ocean had to be on guard the whole time. Otherwise they'd have been thrown overboard and drowned.'

'So when we hear humans boasting about having ancestors on the *Mayflower*, then we can say the same thing!' cried Fletch, excited.

'That's right. We go way back too, and we've made our mark

• 1620 VOYAGE OF THE MAYFLOWER •

here in America. In fact, some say that there are more rats than humans in this country. It makes you feel proud.'

'And I bet those rats and humans must have felt pretty proud - or at least relieved - when the *Mayflower* arrived here in North America. I guess it was quite a trip... it must have taken a week or so?'

'Ha ha! Much, much longer. More like sixty-six days. It's a great story, Fletch.' Norman smiled at his young nephew. 'Here - if you gnaw on this wishbone and sit still, I'll tell you the whole story. The story of the *Mayflower* voyage, that is.'

· ADVENTURES IN THE REAL WORLD ·

• 1620 VOYAGE OF THE MAYFLOWER •

CHAPTER ONE
RELIGIOUS TROUBLES

Both rats settled down while the humans upstairs cleared away plates from their main course. 'So what made those Pilgrims leave England and sail all the way here?' Fletch asked.

Norman could tell that he had an interested audience, and continued the story. 'It all began with an argument about religion. Now we rats are lucky... we just get on with things and don't worry about all that stuff about altars and pews, and kneeling and robes and churches. Humans are different,

• ADVENTURES IN THE REAL WORLD •

though. Especially those humans living in Europe about four or five hundred years ago.

'They took religion really seriously. It could even be a matter of life or death! If you had one set of beliefs and the king or prince had another, then you might be saying goodbye to your head before long.'

'Or tail, if you were a rat?' Fletch clutched his own tail tightly.

'Some rats lost their tails all right, but it wasn't because of religion. It was those stupid humans who think we're the pests. Now where was I? Oh yes....

'For about a thousand years just about everyone in Europe - including England - was of the same religion. They belonged to the Catholic church. Well, around the year of 1500, some people started complaining. They said the Catholic church had lost its way and no longer drew people to God.'

• 1620 VOYAGE OF THE MAYFLOWER •

'So, did they change the church?'

Norman paused. This was going to take some explaining. 'Well, some people felt that the Catholic church needed to be "reformed", or changed. Others, often called "Protestants", felt that it needed to be replaced. And some felt that there wasn't much wrong with the Catholic church and that people should stick with it. So you can see that things were getting a bit complicated and really bad-tempered.'

• ADVENTURES IN THE REAL WORLD •

'And all this stuff was happening in England, too?' asked Fletch, sneaking a quick look up through the cracks, to see if any more food was coming.

'Yes. But for a while everyone remained Catholic. King Henry VIII had "Protestant trouble-makers" put in jail. And the Pope - that's the head of the Catholic church - was so grateful he even gave Henry a special title. The King became known as the "Defender of the Faith".' Norman paused to let that sink in.

'I get it. All this Protestant stuff took place in other European countries but England remained Catholic.'

'Not so fast. Back to Henry. He loved his palaces, sports, hunting and big banquets (mmm, think of all those lovely leftovers)... but he lacked one thing.'

'A head cook to go with him wherever he went? A cuddly pet rat?' Fletch began to stroke an imaginary pet on his lap.

• 1620 VOYAGE OF THE MAYFLOWER •

'No, he had loads of cooks. And pets. What Henry lacked was a son, someone who would become king when he died. He'd been married for years but Catherine, his wife, had given birth to only one child. That was a daughter named Mary. Years went by without a son and Henry began to get desperate. But let's get back to the story.

'Things came to a head in 1534. Henry - remember he was still a Catholic - asked the Pope if he could divorce Catherine. He could then marry Anne Boleyn, a much younger woman, who might well give birth to a boy. The Pope refused, but Henry VIII wouldn't take "no" for an answer. He got Parliament to agree to make him, not the Pope, head of the Church of England.'

Fletch's eyes widened and he muttered, 'So that was that, then, and everyone lived happily ever after?'

'Not so fast! Hold on to your tail. Things get even more complicated. Henry wound up having two more children and

• ADVENTURES IN THE REAL WORLD •

four more wives. After his death in 1547, two of those children became queens and one became king. But each of them controlled how the English people could worship.

THE BREAK WITH ROME

When the Pope refused to let Henry VIII divorce Catherine, the king got the English Parliament to pass a special law. It was called the Act of Supremacy. It made Henry (and all later rulers) head of the Church of England. Henry still viewed himself as a Catholic, but his Church of England got rid of any control by the Pope. If the Church was going to become more Catholic, or more Protestant, it would be mainly down to the king to decide. Royal control became a big part of the Church of England.

• 1620 VOYAGE OF THE MAYFLOWER •

'Anne Boleyn never did give Henry a son, but Henry's third wife, Jane Seymour, did. When he was only nine years old he became King Edward VI when Henry died. Edward's advisers urged him to make the Church of England more Protestant and less like the Catholic church. Then - guess what? - things swung back again.

'Edward VI was never very healthy and he died at the age of sixteen. Stop drumming with that bone, this is serious!'

RELIGIOUS WARS

Most Europeans had to follow the faith - Catholic or Protestant - of their king or prince. Wars were fought between countries whose rulers had different religious beliefs. The Spanish Armada (1588) is the most dramatic example of such a clash. Catholic Spain attacked England, which the Spanish viewed as Protestant. Sometimes the fighting took place within one country. France saw nearly forty years of fighting between Catholics and Protestants until King Henry IV brought peace.

• ADVENTURES IN THE REAL WORLD •

Norman cleared his throat once Fletch stopped drumming. 'So... young Edward died and Henry's daughter Mary became Queen. She wanted to return England to the Catholic faith. Mary was as fierce as her father. She had many leading Protestants executed. That's how she got the nickname "Bloody Mary", although no one would have dared to call her that to her face.

ELIZABETH'S SETTLEMENT

Henry VIII's son, King Edward VI, made the Church of England much more Protestant. After he died, Queen Mary (Catherine's daughter) aimed to make England Catholic. Elizabeth I became queen after Mary's death. She tried to find a middle path in religion. This would stop the swinging back and forth. Elizabeth claimed that she had no 'desire to make windows into men's souls'. She had little patience for those who disagreed, Protestant or Catholic. The Act of Uniformity of 1559 called for punishments for those who didn't fall in step.

• 1620 VOYAGE OF THE MAYFLOWER •

'Like Edward, Mary's reign wasn't long. After just five years as Queen, she died in 1558. And you know what? Things swung back again. Elizabeth, Anne Boleyn's daughter, became Queen Elizabeth I. She was tired of the back-and-forth religious struggles. She tried to find a middle ground. So, the Church of England would have all its prayers and hymns in English (not in Latin, like the Catholic church). Churches would have simple altars, no statues and no stained glass. But priests would still look like Catholic priests, with flowing robes and special headgear.'

'Was Elizabeth the same as "Good Queen Bess"?' Fletch asked.

'Yes. Elizabeth was Queen for 45 years. Most of the religious struggles seemed to have settled down. The English were relieved to have a bit of calm. Many Catholics agreed, even if some still worshipped secretly in the old way. As for the Protestants, some worked to change the Church of England from within. Others, called Separatists, called for a completely new ("separated") Church.

• ADVENTURES IN THE REAL WORLD •

'And some of those Separatists would later become the Pilgrims. Is that all clear?' Norman asked, with a smile.

'Yeah, sure. Would you mind passing me some of that stuffing?'

PURITANS AND SEPARATISTS

Many people wanted to 'purify' the Church of England even more than Elizabeth. They wanted it to become more Protestant. That meant having much simpler forms of worship. These 'Puritans' had no desire to form their own religion. Others felt that the Church of England couldn't be purified. These 'Separatists' called for a new Church. A leading Separatist, Robert Browne, inspired the group who would set sail on the Mayflower. Scrooby, Nottinghamshire, became a centre of Separatism.

• ADVENTURES IN THE REAL WORLD •

24

• 1620 VOYAGE OF THE MAYFLOWER •

CHAPTER TWO
TESTING THE WATERS

Fletch could hear the humans serving more food upstairs. He smiled. Soon more bits and pieces would be coming his way. But he could wait because he was getting really interested in his uncle's story. Interested and curious. So he asked:

'When did Good Queen Bess finally die? I'm all ears.'

• ADVENTURES IN THE REAL WORLD •

Norman chuckled and looked across at his nephew: 'All tummy, more like it. You're stuffed with stuffing by the look of you. Now, where was I? Oh, yes, Good Queen Bess. She died in 1603, and the English were very sad.'

'Did another queen take over?'

Norman smiled, because Fletch really did seem interested.

'Elizabeth never married. That's why they called her "the Virgin Queen". But not getting married also meant she had no children to take over and be the next queen or king.'

'So if they didn't have anyone sitting on that big, big throne in London - who got to rule over everyone?' Fletch was getting confused. What did all this stuff about kings and queens in England have to do with those Pilgrims?

'They got a king instead. It turns out that the King of Scotland, James, was related to Henry VIII. So he got to

• 1620 VOYAGE OF THE MAYFLOWER •

be King of Scotland and England. He became King James I of England. Oh - before I forget - Scotland was mainly a Protestant country by then. So, as you'd expect, the English Catholics weren't happy to have a Protestant King.'

Fletch wanted to show that he'd been paying attention: 'But those Separatists must have been pleased, right?'

'Uh, not really. It was all quite complicated because although James was a Protestant, he was now King of England. And that meant that he was in charge of the Church of England. He took that role very seriously. And he wasn't pleased to have Catholics or Separatists in his kingdom, while he was in charge of the Church of England.'

Norman made a serious face, and paused. Fletch stopped thinking of food. He imagined what sort of horrible punishments the Separatists might have faced back then. Norman gave Fletch time to think, then he continued:

• ADVENTURES IN THE REAL WORLD •

'Things got so tough that some Separatists decided to pack their bags and sail away.'

'To America?'

'Wrong - to Holland.'

Fletch looked really confused again. 'Erm, correct me if I'm wrong, but isn't that completely the wrong way? Going east rather than west?'

Norman sighed. 'You're right. Holland is to the east and America is to the west. The boldest English Separatists had begun to worship openly in the village of Scrooby in Nottinghamshire. They couldn't worship in the local church because it was against the law. So they would meet in houses. One belonged to an important local man, William Brewster.

'Brewster would invite a Separatist preacher, John Smyth, to hold services. People had to keep a look-out for soldiers who might come to arrest them. Some Separatists wound up in jail. Others had to pay big fines. They were finding it harder and harder to live in England because of their beliefs. So they had two choices...'

Fletch piped up: 'Stay in England and get punished or go somewhere safer!'

TROUBLE FROM ALL SIDES

It's hard to imagine what it was like to worship secretly. It was against the law to worship anywhere but in an official church. And 'official' meant the Church of England, with the King (or Queen) at its head. The English Separatists knew that the forces of the King hunted down anyone who didn't obey the law. Even worse was the hatred that Separatists felt from their neighbours. People would hear stories at church, week after week, about how evil Separatists were. Neighbours would turn against former friends if those friends chose to ignore the national church.

• ADVENTURES IN THE REAL WORLD •

• 1620 VOYAGE OF THE MAYFLOWER •

31

• ADVENTURES IN THE REAL WORLD •

• 1620 VOYAGE OF THE MAYFLOWER •

'Exactly! But even that choice got trickier. Around this time, in the early 1600s, England had begun its first settlement in North America. It was called Jamestown, after the new King. And the area around it, or colony, was to be called Virginia. That name honoured Queen Elizabeth ("the Virgin Queen").'

Fletch butted in: 'Ah... so the Separatists started packing for a voyage to Virginia, right? Bring on the *Mayflower*!'

OLD AND NEW WORLDS

European voyages to the New World were becoming more common by the early 1600s. Christopher Columbus, an Italian sailor hired by the Spanish, had crossed the Atlantic in 1492. Within a few years, Spain had claimed much of Central America and most of South America. The Portuguese, English, French, Swedish and Dutch followed the Spanish example. By 1600, much of North America's east coast was claimed by one of those European countries. But very few Europeans had actually moved there.

• ADVENTURES IN THE REAL WORLD •

'Once again, not so simple,' explained Norman. 'The settlement in Virginia was very loyal to the Church of England. Separatists wouldn't be welcomed there.'

'I get it,' said Fletch. But he didn't really get it. As he saw it, the Separatists were minding their own business in England, but the King's men kept arresting them. They weren't wanted in Virginia, either, by the sound of it. Where could they turn?

VIRGINIA

England's first permanent colony in North America was called Virginia. It was named after Queen Elizabeth I, England's 'Virgin Queen'. The colony was founded in 1607, four years after Elizabeth had died. But English explorers and fishermen had visited the area since the 1580s. From the start, Virginia was settled by English people who were happy with the Church of England. It would have been a difficult place for Separatists, who wanted to abandon that Church.

Norman could see how puzzled Fletch was. 'You're probably thinking, "Where could the Separatists turn?".'

'Exactly. You read my mind. They had absolutely nowhere to go, did they?'

Norman smiled patiently. 'Well, they did have one place to go, and I think I mentioned it before. It's not nearly as far away as America.'

'Holland?' Fletch thought he was right, but wasn't sure.

'That's right. Protestant Holland, or the Netherlands, was winning its independence from Catholic Spain. The Dutch could now practice their faith freely. And they could welcome other Protestants like the English Separatists. So that's what led them to Holland - after one or two false starts when the King's men stopped them from leaving.

'In Holland the Separatists could gather together freely for their services. No royal troops would bother them anymore. It really was a chance to start all over, in safety. Their new home was in the Dutch city of Leiden.'

DUTCH INDEPENDENCE

The Dutch had been ruled by Spain from the early 1500s. They weren't happy under Spanish control. Things got even worse when most Dutch people turned to the Protestant faith. Spain was the most powerful Catholic country in Europe. It clamped down on Protestants in the Netherlands. That led to a revolt. The Netherlands had to wait until 1648 to gain full independence. But by 1589 the Dutch had thrown off most Spanish control. And the Protestant Netherlands soon became very attractive to English Separatists.

• 1620 VOYAGE OF THE MAYFLOWER •

Poor Fletch still looked puzzled. 'So why don't we hear about Leiden Rock instead of Plymouth Rock? And why aren't you and I munching on those delicious Dutch cheeses like Gouda and Edam... instead of all these lovely Thanksgiving leftovers?'

• ADVENTURES IN THE REAL WORLD •

'Mainly for one reason: homesickness. Those newcomers were Separatists, but they were English Separatists... and they began to get homesick. Some of their children could speak Dutch better than English, others were old enough to join the Dutch army or even marry their Dutch neighbours.

'The Separatists began to think again about the New World. America was said to be a huge place, after all. Maybe they could find somewhere to settle far from the Virginia Royalists, the people loyal to the Church of England. So, can you see that they're getting a little closer to Plymouth now?'

• ADVENTURES IN THE REAL WORLD •

'Hmmm. I suppose so. But I'm still thinking about all that Dutch cheese they'd be leaving behind. And don't the Dutch make delicious sweet waffles, too?'

'I'm sure that the Separatists could make their own cheese. And they probably knew the recipe for making waffles. But by now they were itching to sail across the Atlantic. They wanted to create their own settlement. The Dutch weren't stopping them. But there were two small matters to consider: how to cross the Atlantic, and how to pay for the voyage.'

• ADVENTURES IN THE REAL WORLD •

42

• ADVENTURES IN THE REAL WORLD •

• 1620 VOYAGE OF THE MAYFLOWER •

CHAPTER THREE
A 'PROSPEROUS WIND'

Norman could see that Fletch wanted to hear about the famous voyage itself. But first there was a smaller voyage to describe.

'The Separatists had saved some money while living in Leiden. They decided to use it to buy a ship called the *Speedwell* to take them across the Atlantic Ocean. Meanwhile, they learned that other Separatists - still in England - also wanted to make the crossing. It was unlikely that the extra folk would fit on their small ship...'

• ADVENTURES IN THE REAL WORLD •

'So the people in England had to buy their own ship!' Fletch was getting excited now, and was marching back and forth like a sailor on parade.

'Well, that wasn't so easy. The Separatists were scattered through different parts of England. Besides, they probably couldn't scrape together enough money to let them buy a ship of their own.'

'So what happened - did they give up? One group has a ship, except it's not called the *Mayflower*. The other group, in England, can't get a ship. And what about all our ancestors - all the English rats who were packing for the long journey?'

Norman laughed. He wondered what foods the English rats might have packed. Or would they feast on scraps, like all those rats on the Navy's large ships?

'The English Separatists knew that other people would be willing to pay for the journey across the Atlantic. Companies

• 1620 VOYAGE OF THE MAYFLOWER •

in England were already making money from such trips.

'People called investors pooled their money together into these companies. One, known as the Virginia Company, learned about the Separatists' plans in 1620. Thomas Weston arranged for a ship to carry the Separatists to North America. The money for the ship and the voyage would come from the company. But the Separatists would have to pay it back once they were in America. Oh, I almost forgot to say - the name of the ship was the *Mayflower*.'

'Hooray! Finally!' Fletch sat up. 'So when did they sail?'

'Well, don't forget that the Separatists had two ships, one in the Netherlands and one in England. The Leiden group would sail on the *Speedwell* to join the English group. Then both would set sail together.

'And that's exactly what happened - at least the first bit. On 22nd July 1620, the Leiden group set sail on the *Speedwell*,

• ADVENTURES IN THE REAL WORLD •

bound for the port of Southampton on England's south coast. And that's where the other Separatists and the *Mayflower* would be waiting. The *Mayflower*, with about 65 on board, had left London for Southampton a week earlier.

SPONSORING SETTLEMENTS

Companies in London and other English cities came up with money to form new settlements in North America. These companies would find people, called investors, to pay for voyages. In return, they expected to get their money back many times over. The people in the new settlements would repay their debts by sending valuable things back to England. Rich people in Europe would pay lots of money for beaver hats, for example. North America had what seemed like an endless supply of beavers and other fur-covered animals. It seemed like 'easy money' for investors but the risks were high. Their ships might sink in storms or be attacked by pirates. And maybe the English settlers would be wiped out by cold, disease or attacks by Native Americans?

• 1620 VOYAGE OF THE MAYFLOWER •

'Imagine the excitement when the two groups met up. Old friends saw each other for the first time in years. For some of the Leiden group, this was their first time in England. Everyone was speaking English and all the signs were in their own language. But the Separatists had to take care. After all, they were still not welcome in their own land.

'Plus, this would be their last time in comfortable beds and warm houses. What lay in wait on the long voyage ahead of them? And what would await them on the other side of the great ocean?

'Those same worries - about the voyage and harsh conditions in America - had another effect. In those days, people believed that girls and women were weaker than boys and men. Many feared that their women and girls wouldn't survive. So they left them behind with relatives. Some stayed in Leiden and others remained in England. The Separatists hoped that they'd make the trip to join them in America once things got settled there.

• ADVENTURES IN THE REAL WORLD •

'Remember the name William Brewster? He was one of the leading Separatists when they were worshipping secretly. He prepared to make the crossing along with his two sons, Love and Wrestling.'

Fletch grinned. 'Wrestling? What a great name for a boy! Did they have a brother named Football?'

'No, but they had two sisters called Patience and Fear who stayed behind. Other fathers did the same. Francis Cooke took his son John along, but left behind two daughters: Jane and Hester. Richard Warren's five daughters, aged between two and ten - Mary, Ann, Sarah, Elizabeth and Abigail - would all remain in England. Another Mary and Sarah - Degory Priest's daughters - were also left behind. Thomas Rogers and his son Joseph packed their things, but not Joseph's sisters Elizabeth and Margaret. None of those girls could make the trip because of their father's worries.'

'Did any girls and women go on the first trip?'

• 1620 VOYAGE OF THE MAYFLOWER •

'Oh, some did. One of them - Humility Cooper - was just one year old. Her mother had died, so her uncle and aunt took her with them to the New World. And some older girls, like teenagers Elizabeth Tilley and Desire Minter, were welcome because they were already helpful members of their family.

'In fact, the young girls who went over to America seemed to get by better than the boys and all the adults. Fewer young girls died during the harsh first winter. But I'm jumping ahead... back to our story. It's still late July 1620 and both sets of Separatists are ready to leave their home country to start a new life in the New World.'

Fletch's eyes flashed. 'Ahoy, mates! Get ready to hoist sails. Make sure the rats on board are comfortable!'

'I don't think the sailors worried about the rats. And I'm sure the rats didn't expect kindness from the humans either. On 5th August 1620, the *Speedwell* and *Mayflower* set sail from Southampton.'

• ADVENTURES IN THE REAL WORLD •

'Next stop... the New World!' Fletch announced.

'Er... not exactly. The next stop happened to be Dartmouth, back on the English south coast. The *Speedwell* had sprung some leaks and had to be repaired back at port. Everyone had to wait, stuck on board going nowhere, for another week. Then the two ships set off again on 21st August.'

Fletch was pacing up and down, like a sailor on the lookout for land in the distance. 'What's this? Land ho!'

'Well... the sailors did sight land, but I'm afraid it was back in England again. The *Speedwell* sprang more leaks when the ships had gone about 483 km (300 miles). Both ships had to return to port again. This time they arrived in Plymouth.'

'Plymouth! Hurrah! Finally! That voyage didn't take too long.' Fletch's smile began to fade when Norman sighed.

'I don't think you've been paying attention. It wasn't this

• 1620 VOYAGE OF THE MAYFLOWER •

Plymouth, here in America, where they wound up. It was Plymouth in England. And this time it looked as though there was no hope for the *Speedwell*.

THE SPEEDWELL MYSTERY

Everyone agreed that the Speedwell, the ship that was meant to join the Mayflower, had begun to leak badly. It would have been risky sailing her very far from the English shore, and a trip across the Atlantic would be a disaster. But did the leaks just develop naturally? Some people crowded onto the Mayflower thought that they might have been done on purpose. The crew of the Speedwell was already worried about making the crossing so late in the year. They might all starve to death in the cold American winter. Maybe it was safer to spring a few leaks and remain safely in England?

• ADVENTURES IN THE REAL WORLD •

'Some of the passengers decided that enough was enough and gave up. The rest of them decided to squeeze into the *Mayflower* and make the trip with one ship. So, on 6th September 1620, the *Mayflower* finally set sail from Plymouth. As William Bradford wrote in his account, years later, the *Mayflower* had finally found "a prosperous wind".

'But think about the time of year. The days are getting shorter and colder. Winds are picking up. You can imagine how rough the seas would be. And imagine landing a couple of months later in a strange place, with the days getting even shorter and winter coming. Plus, they'd have to build their own houses when they got there.'

Fletch shivered, even though there was still a lot of warmth coming from upstairs. 'I wouldn't have liked to set off on a journey across the Atlantic at that time of year. And in a rickety little ship with waves washing over the deck and the wind tearing at the sails. Just think of the poor rats who'd gone along for the ride.'

• 1620 VOYAGE OF THE MAYFLOWER •

SAINTS AND STRANGERS

The merchant investors didn't bank on a group of religious extremists being able to make a profit in the New World so they sent a number of able-bodied men to help with the practical side of setting up the colony and trading. The term 'pilgrim' wasn't used as the term to describe the Separatists on board; instead they were called 'saints'. The others were 'strangers'. Despite their differences, the two groups knew that they would be relying on each other. That applied to the difficult voyage and to starting a new life in the New World.

Norman thought about his nephew for a few moments. He was kind, and would grow up to be a good rat. He was proud of him, but he had to point out that there aren't many accounts of the rats on board the *Mayflower*.

• ADVENTURES IN THE REAL WORLD •

'Fletch, you're a kind-hearted rat. It's good that you thought of our ancestors so long ago. We can only imagine what the journey was like for them. But we do have some good accounts of life for the humans. I've been calling them Separatists up to now, because that's how other English people described them at the time. But over the years we've come to know them as Pilgrims. So now that they've set sail from England, that's what I'll call them.'

The young rat was glowing after his uncle's praise. And he was getting more and more interested in the story now that the rats (and the Pilgrims) were finally on their way. First he wanted to know a little bit more about the ship.

'Uncle Norman, just how big was the *Mayflower*? Did the passengers all have cabins? And what about the rats?'

'It wasn't a very big ship at all. Only about 100 feet long. Nothing like the big ocean liners nowadays. But although it was short, the ship had tall cabins fore and aft.'

• 1620 VOYAGE OF THE MAYFLOWER •

'Four and what?' Fletch didn't understand.

Norman smiled. 'Not F-O-U-R, Fletch, F-O-R-E! It's a different word and it means the front. A bit like the word "before".'

'So "aft" must mean the back of the ship, like the word "after"?'

'That's right. These tall bits of the ship were almost like little houses. But they weren't for passengers. They protected the crew from wind and rain and waves.

'In fact, the ship wasn't even built to carry passengers. The *Mayflower* had already worked for years as a cargo ship. That meant that it was used to carry goods like wool and grain from one port to another. It was used mainly to take wine from France to England.

'But being a cargo ship, the *Mayflower* had some advantages for the journey. Although it was not very long, it was wide. So the area below the deck could also hold lots of goods. The

• ADVENTURES IN THE REAL WORLD •

company paying for the journey wanted the new settlement to succeed. That meant packing lots of things to help the settlers get started in America.

DESTINATION VIRGINIA

The Mayflower was aiming for the colony of Virginia, which was much larger than today's state of the same name. It extended up to the Hudson River (near present-day New York City). The Pilgrims had heard good reports of living in Virginia. And they had permission to settle in its northern edge, near the Hudson. They would still be living in Virginia, but several hundred miles north of the main settlement in Jamestown. The Pilgrims felt that they'd be well away from anyone trying to force them to be part of the Church of England.

'But guess what having all that space for goods meant? All the passengers had to squeeze into the areas meant for storing barrels and boxes. I mean the human passengers, of course.

• 1620 VOYAGE OF THE MAYFLOWER •

The rats were fine. They could nibble into sacks of grain and hide in corners that the humans couldn't reach.'

Fletch was pleased that the rats probably had a better journey than the humans. But he still wanted to learn a lot more about the Pilgrims.

'Uncle, nowadays we are always hearing about people whose ancestors came over on the *Mayflower*. There must have been hundreds of them, if these people are telling the truth.'

This time it was Norman's turn to open his eyes wide. He was about to surprise Fletch. 'You might think that there were hundreds of Pilgrims on board. But I can tell you that the number was much smaller. All in all, there were 102 passengers on board the *Mayflower*, and less than half of them were Pilgrims. The rest were servants, crew members or craftsmen (called "strangers" or "sinners" by the Pilgrims) that the investor's company had decided to send along to help create a new settlement.

• ADVENTURES IN THE REAL WORLD •

'The first few weeks of the crossing were calm. But most of the passengers had never been on a ship before. And a lot of them soon began to feel...'

'Seasick!' Fletch was looking a little green himself. He had probably eaten too much cranberry sauce.

'That's right. And some of the sailors would tease them when they started to look a little green and...'

'I know what you're going to say. But with the ship rocking back and forth, and big waves crashing, where could they throw up?'

Norman began to look a little green himself as he explained. 'They had slop buckets down between decks, where the Pilgrims had to stay during the voyage. So they used the buckets if they had to throw up or... well, for anything else really, if you see what I mean? They had no toilets.'

· 1620 VOYAGE OF THE MAYFLOWER ·

'You mean they used the slop buckets for that too?!' Now it was Fletch's turn to look disgusted.

• ADVENTURES IN THE REAL WORLD •

'Yes, and if the weather was rough, then the buckets had to stay between decks too. They could only be emptied if the sea was calm. And, of course, there was all that waste from the animals to deal with, too.'

Fletch looked annoyed. 'Please, uncle - not just any old ordinary "animals". You're talking about our ancestors - the most important animals of all: rats!'

'No, I really do mean animals - quite a lot of them actually. Some families took along pets, like cats and birds. At least two passengers had hunting dogs with them. The *Mayflower* also carried chickens, sheep, pigs and goats. The children helped look after the animals. But the animals' pails also needed to be emptied.' Norman held his nose at the thought.

'Can you imagine trying to sleep with that smell? And the constant rocking and swaying. Candles and oil lamps gave a bit of light, but think of the danger! If one of those tipped over a wooden ship could easily go up in flames! Passengers had

• 1620 VOYAGE OF THE MAYFLOWER •

to share one big cabin so people hung sheets inbetween to get a little privacy. Some people managed to string hammocks between beams, but lots of Pilgrims had to sleep on the bare floor. That was life during the long dark nights. But the days dragged on too.

'The sailors and "sinners" played cards to kill time. But the Pilgrims didn't approve of card games. They spent a lot of time praying. Some of the children had dolls and small toys like spinning tops. People read, played riddling games or told stories. The children loved to hear stories about America. Some of the sailors and at least one Pilgrim had already been there. The children learned about bears and wolves and about people there who wore hardly any clothing and painted their bodies.'

Fletch was looking a little less green, and beginning to feel slightly hungry again. He could smell more food from the feast upstairs. 'Mmmm. You know, I'm still feeling a little peckish. What did the Pilgrims eat on the *Mayflower?*'

• ADVENTURES IN THE REAL WORLD •

'Nothing like the feast upstairs, Fletch. Everyone - including children - drank beer. They had dried meat and salted fish, a bit of cheese, some dried fruit plus something called hardtack. That was a biscuit made of flour and water, and sometimes a little salt.'

'That list sounds fine for us rats but don't humans like to cook most of their food? I can hear the oven door opening and closing upstairs all the time. Did the Pilgrims cook anything? Or... could they, on a ship?'

Fletch really was paying attention. Norman began to describe something that was just as dangerous as the burning lamps and the candles.

'Everyone ate together in groups. And yes, they did cook some of their food. But it was tricky, because it was cooked in fireboxes right in the middle of the ship. That's the bit of the ship they called the waist, just as our waists are in the middle of our bodies.

• 1620 VOYAGE OF THE MAYFLOWER •

'The firebox was a pretty basic way of cooking. It was a metal box that rested on beams along the floor. It was filled with sand so it looked a little like a child's sandpit. And people would light fires on the sand to cook. Everyone had a daily ration, or portion, of food.

BIRTH AND DEATH

Midway across the Atlantic, Stephen Hopkins began to fear for his wife Elizabeth. He knew that she was due to give birth to a child, but he thought the baby would come once they arrived in America. His wife's loud groaning told him that the birth was going to be much sooner. So, there on the Mayflower, she gave birth to a little boy and named him Oceanus. The Mayflower also lost a passenger along the way. William Burton, a servant, became severely ill and died. He was buried at sea, which means that his body was thrown overboard.

• 1620 VOYAGE OF THE MAYFLOWER •

'All in all, conditions were difficult for the entire journey. Even when the seas were calm, passengers struggled with boredom. But they didn't want things to get too calm! Remember that the *Mayflower* was a sailing ship. It needed wind in its sails to go anywhere. Passengers had heard stories of ships that had been "becalmed". With no wind, they just drifted for days... as all their supplies slowly ran out.

'One of the most dramatic events of the voyage took place in a storm. John Howland, a servant, got swept overboard. On most days that would have been certain death as the ship would simply have sailed on. But the rough weather probably saved Howland. Very strong winds could have torn the ship's sail or caused a mast to snap. So the captain had ordered the sails to be dropped. Instead of being blown forward, the *Mayflower* bobbed up and down on the rough seas like a cork. So the crew was able to throw a line out for Howland to grab and he was hauled to safety.'

• ADVENTURES IN THE REAL WORLD •

Fletch's eyes opened wide with excitement. 'Wow, what a great story that is!'

'But that's not the end of it. Saving that servant probably changed history. Rowland went on to marry and have children, and three of his descendants eventually became US Presidents: Franklin Roosevelt, George H. W. Bush and his son George W. Bush.

'Just after sunrise on 9th November 1620, after more than two months of boredom, excitement, terror, one birth and one death, the *Mayflower* sailors spotted land. They had reached the New World. But there was one slight problem: they were 322 km (200 miles) from where they should have been!'

• **1620 VOYAGE OF THE MAYFLOWER** •

SENT TO BE SERVANTS

The marriage between the Shropshire couple Samuel More and his wife Katherine had ended in divorce. Samuel wound up in control of the four young children – Ellen, Jasper, Richard and Mary. Another man had been their father, so Samuel decided to send them away to America. He saw that some Mayflower passengers were looking for children to train as servants, so he paid for them to be shipped to America with a group of 'honest and religious' Separatists. Richard and Mary were placed with William Brewster. Jasper joined John Carver and Ellen joined Edward Winslow. Only Richard survived the first winter, but one of his descendants is familiar to everyone: George Washington.

• ADVENTURES IN THE REAL WORLD •

• 1620 VOYAGE OF THE MAYFLOWER •

CHAPTER FOUR

ANOTHER VOYAGE?

The *Mayflower* had definitely reached the coast of North America, but it was by the tip of Cape Cod. That's far to the north of its target, near the mouth of the Hudson River. Jamestown, the capital of Virginia, was unfortunately over 322 km (200 miles) south of that.

• ADVENTURES IN THE REAL WORLD •

'Christopher Jones, the *Mayflower*'s captain, decided to sail on. He wanted to make it to the Hudson. But the weather turned poor and the ship was turned back. The *Mayflower* was nearly shipwrecked. So the captain ordered it to sail back around the tip of Cape Cod and into a sheltered harbour.'

CAPE COD

Most people know of Cape Cod because of beach holidays, whale watching and excellent seafood. And its unforgettable shape, like the flexed arm, figures on many postcards. But for sailors – even today – the waters around the peninsula can be deadly. Shifting sands and strong currents make it very hard to stay on course. The ocean floor around 'the Cape' is littered with shipwrecks. Captain Jones's decision to sail back to what's now Provincetown might well have saved the Mayflower.

• 1620 VOYAGE OF THE MAYFLOWER •

Fletch was getting excited again. 'So the *Mayflower* had reached Plymouth! Did they start building houses?'

'Not so fast, Fletch. Remember how the voyage began with some false starts? Well, it ended in much the same way. Cape Cod extends more than 100 km (62 miles) out into the wild Atlantic. The Pilgrims had landed in a harbour just inside the end of the Cape. Nowadays we know that by the name of Provincetown Harbour.'

Fletch was on his back, wriggling his legs this way and that.

'Fletch, what are you doing? What's wrong with you?'

'I'm trying to flex my legs to look like Cape Cod. But I don't think rat legs are built for it!'

'No, they're not. But think about the rats on board the *Mayflower*. Do you suppose some of them might have sneaked up on to the deck? They probably wanted to find out

• ADVENTURES IN THE REAL WORLD •

where they'd be living. Think of what they would have seen when they first arrived. Instead of rolling fields and rippling streams, there was sand nearly everywhere around them. A few small pine trees grew crookedly. The trees were probably blown sideways into those funny angles by the constant very strong winds.

'Meanwhile the humans had some real thinking to do. They had finally crossed the ocean, but they weren't where they were supposed to be, which wasn't so good. On the other hand, they were even further from the snooping folk down in Virginia, which wasn't so bad. It meant that they wouldn't get into trouble because of their beliefs.

'If they were going to stay outside Virginia, they'd have to ask the King for permission to set up a new colony. But before they could do that, they faced a serious problem. Arguments had broken out on board, even before the *Mayflower* had lowered anchor in the harbour.'

• 1620 VOYAGE OF THE MAYFLOWER •

Fletch had straightened his legs again and looked more comfortable. 'I guess everyone got a bit cooped up on the trip. Stuck with the same people for two months with no escape. I'd scream if I'd been with my own brother for that long. No wonder the Pilgrims started arguing among themselves.'

'No, the Pilgrims weren't arguing. It was the folk who weren't Pilgrims - the ones that the Pilgrims called "sinners" - who got fed up. They'd had enough of that religious group. Some of them were threatening to go off on their own when they landed. After all, they were beyond the reach of those in charge of Virginia.'

'So what happened? Was there a big fight on board the *Mayflower*?'

'No. William Bradford and other Pilgrims decided to write an official document. It was called the *Mayflower Compact*. That became well known in American history. First of all,

• ADVENTURES IN THE REAL WORLD •

the *Compact* was a way of saying to the "sinners" that all *Mayflower* passengers needed to work together. It also showed that the people signing it remained loyal to the English King. But most importantly, it spelled out some of the ways that the people would govern themselves.

'Forty-one adult men signed the document. Women and children didn't count, so they couldn't sign it.'

• **1620 VOYAGE OF THE MAYFLOWER** •

DECLARATION OF INDEPENDENCE?

The Mayflower Compact promised that a new Pilgrim colony would remain loyal to the English King. But it also stated something shocking for the time. It said its authority, the reason it would be obeyed, came from the people themselves. Although the year was still only 1620, it paved the way for independence in America. Many people now see it as a first step towards America's famous Declaration of Independence in 1776. Other parts of North America, notably Quebec (French), Virginia (British) and Mexico (Spanish), were settled by Europeans before the Pilgrims even set sail from England. Unlike the Pilgrims, none of them took any early steps towards becoming independent of their 'mother countries' back in Europe.

'Let me guess, I bet that not a single rat was asked to sign that piece of paper, either?' It was hard to tell whether Fletch was just joking or really angry.

• ADVENTURES IN THE REAL WORLD •

'Yes, once again, the rats were not asked to take part. Maybe it's because the humans had other things on their mind. For one thing, they needed to find fresh water, firewood, food of some sort and a place to start building a settlement. A soldier named Myles Standish led two scouting missions out from the harbour. About fifteen men joined him on each mission. The first was on foot and on the second they took a small boat to explore the shore near them.

FIRST ENCOUNTER BEACH

Holiday-makers on Cape Cod enjoy the sheltered waters of First Encounter Beach. It takes its name from the first meeting (or 'encounter') between the Pilgrims and Native Americans. Myles Standish's scouting party had travelled a few miles south of the harbour where the Mayflower was moored. They were looking for water, food and maybe a good spot to build their settlement. They found springs and some woodland but nowhere suitable to settle. A brief attack from the local Nauset (Native Americans) convinced them to look somewhere else.

• ADVENTURES IN THE REAL WORLD •

'Standish's men found traces of villages that had belonged to the Nauset people. They were the local Native Americans. The English would camp each night, either behind fallen trees or inside their small boat. A surprise attack by Nauset warriors woke them one night. A few shots were fired, but fortunately no one was injured.

• 1620 VOYAGE OF THE MAYFLOWER •

'The two missions, plus the unfriendly welcome, convinced the Pilgrims that they should build their settlement somewhere else. They knew of a stretch of shore across the bay called New Plymouth. That seemed like a good place to end a voyage that began in Old Plymouth.'

• ADVENTURES IN THE REAL WORLD •

FINAL VOYAGE

After all the stops, starts and changes of course, the Mayflower's final voyage was the short, 64 kilometre (40-mile) crossing of Massachusetts Bay. Several people on board knew a bit about the mainland on the other side of the bay. They described a large sheltered harbour, with meadows and woodland going down to the shore. That sounded a lot more promising than the sand dunes and thin woodland of Cape Cod. Captain John Smith, from the Virginia settlement, had visited that stretch of coast before 1620. He had named it New Plymouth. The Pilgrims were happy to keep the name since they had sailed from 'old' Plymouth.

84

• 1620 VOYAGE OF THE MAYFLOWER •

• ADVENTURES IN THE REAL WORLD •

86

• 1620 VOYAGE OF THE MAYFLOWER •

CHAPTER FIVE

THE HARSH WINTER

OK, Fletch. You've been paying attention so far. Now it's time for a question. Have you ever heard of Forefathers Day?'

'Oh, that's easy! That's the big holiday here in Plymouth just before Christmas. There's usually a feast for the humans. Not as big as Thanksgiving, but with lots of scraps for us rats.'

• ADVENTURES IN THE REAL WORLD •

'Yes, it's that celebration just before Christmas. On 21st December, to be exact. Two more questions. Do you know why it's always on that date? And what does "forefathers" mean?'

'Umm... "forefathers" means people in the past, doesn't it? And the date is, um, the first day of winter?'

'Close, with both. Forefathers are people who lived in a place long, long ago. Maybe even our great-great-great-great grandparents. I might even have left out a few "greats" just now. And you're right that 21st December is the beginning of winter, but that's not the point of Forefathers Day.

'The holiday marks the day, on the 21st December 1620, when the *Mayflower* finally arrived here in Plymouth, not at Cape Cod. Remember that the Pilgrims didn't think that the end of Cape Cod was a good place to build their houses.

'It turns out that they weren't the first settlers in Plymouth where we are now.'

• 1620 VOYAGE OF THE MAYFLOWER •

TOUGH CONDITIONS

The Pilgrim settlement at Plymouth is in what is now called the state of Massachusetts. The soil there is not as rich as it is in Virginia, where the Pilgrims were heading. Plus, winter temperatures can remain below freezing for weeks on end. Snow covers the ground for months. It's easy to see how hard it was to arrive with no fresh food on the first day of a long winter!

Fletch sat up straight. 'Of course! I bet loads of rats already lived there. And that they were ready to welcome the English rats to the shore.'

'I'm sure that there were lots of rats. But I'm talking about people, human beings. That part of the Massachusetts coast was a good place for people to build a settlement. It had a good harbour. Well, you know all this because you live here! But in those days, when there weren't cars and telephones

• ADVENTURES IN THE REAL WORLD •

and paving, the land looked different. Gentle fields led down to the water. Low hills to the west protected the coast and the harbour from the coldest winds. Freshwater streams ran down from the hills.

'And for that reason, the Wampanoag Native Americans had built a village right there, more than a hundred years before the Pilgrims arrived. The village - and the people who lived there - were called Patuxet. But a serious illness had swept across Patuxet just two years before the Pilgrims arrived. The Patuxet people had left.'

'So that means that the Pilgrims found houses to move into?'

'Not exactly. The Native Americans who lived along the coast didn't build permanent homes. They lived in wigwams, which were like tents made from branches and animal skins. A wigwam wouldn't last more than a year or so. And by the time the Pilgrims arrived, the wigwams had either collapsed under snow or blown away.

• 1620 VOYAGE OF THE MAYFLOWER •

'Still, the Pilgrims, like the Patuxet people, saw that the location was ideal. And it was already cleared for them. But they still had to build everything from scratch.'

Fletch brightened. 'That must have been fun. Building your own village!'

• ADVENTURES IN THE REAL WORLD •

'Not at all. As you know 21st December was the start of winter and that was the day that the Pilgrims arrived. It became known as "the Killing Winter". Only about half of the *Mayflower* passengers would live to see another winter.

FOOD LESSONS

Many of the Pilgrims were farmers. They thought that they'd be able to produce food for themselves. But conditions were not at all like England, or even Virginia. They had never even heard of the area's main crop, maize. Luckily some local Native Americans gave them advice about farming. The Pilgrims learned how to use dead fish to enrich the soil. That helped them grow maize and other crops. They also saw how the sea could provide food. Each tide revealed hundreds of herring and other fish, as well as lobster and shellfish. Without this knowledge the Pilgrims would not have lasted through 'the Killing Winter'.

• 1620 VOYAGE OF THE MAYFLOWER •

'Within days the Pilgrims began work on a building where many families could live together. Men and boys would work on land during the day and return to the ship at night. Women and girls stayed on the *Mayflower*.'

• ADVENTURES IN THE REAL WORLD •

DISEASES

The Mayflower passengers were stuck on board all through the winter. The conditions were just as cramped as they were during the voyage. But now people had to face the Massachusetts winter. The lamps and fireboxes threw out a little heat, but not much. People became ill. Even something as typical as a common cold could turn deadly. Living so close to one another meant that diseases spread quickly through the ship. Only 47 of the 102 passengers were still alive when spring came. The dead included John Carver, who was elected governor back when the Mayflower Compact was signed. William Bradford was elected the new governor.

Fletch darkened again. 'That would have driven me crazy, especially after such a long voyage.'

• 1620 VOYAGE OF THE MAYFLOWER •

'We don't know whether anyone went crazy, but many people became ill. And supplies of food were running out. I'm afraid lots of Pilgrims died. Those who survived had to work that much harder to build their settlement.

'Boys did help their fathers build the first houses, but it can't have been fun. They had to help drag logs in from the woods and carry tools to help build houses, fences and a fort. Work began on the first building on Christmas Day, 1620. It became a common house, where people could gather. It would also be home for families until their own houses were built.'

• ADVENTURES IN THE REAL WORLD •

'No central heating. No hot baths. No comfy beds, and starting work on Christmas Day. That's definitely not how people spend Christmas here in Plymouth nowadays.' Fletch shivered as he thought of those early days in Plymouth.

• 1620 VOYAGE OF THE MAYFLOWER •

NEIGHBOURS

The English weren't the first people to settle in North America. Native Americans had lived there for thousands of years. Like the Europeans, they formed many different nations. Some people call those nations tribes. And also like the Europeans, some of these nations fought each other. The Patuxet people who lived near Plymouth were part of the Wampanoag nation. These people were curious about the new arrivals from across the sea. One of the first buildings in Plymouth was a fort. The Pilgrims weren't sure whether their neighbours would treat them like friends or deadly enemies.

• ADVENTURES IN THE REAL WORLD •

100

• 1620 VOYAGE OF THE MAYFLOWER •

CHAPTER SIX

HELPING HANDS

Fletch had some questions. 'Uncle Norman, did the rest of the Pilgrims die out in the second year? Or did they last? I guess they must have because we still talk about them. And there's all those humans who brag about being "*Mayflower* descendants"… so some of them must have survived. But how? I don't get it.'

'You could say they were lucky. But the luckiest thing was getting to know their Wampanoag neighbours. Remember Myles Standish and the scouting parties when the *Mayflower* landed on Cape Cod?'

• ADVENTURES IN THE REAL WORLD •

'Yes, they came across some Native Americans then. Didn't they have a fight?'

'Sort of. Those Nauset people had strong ties with the Wampanoag on the mainland. The "fight" was nothing more than Standish and his men firing muskets. But the scouting party had already angered the locals when they had found some buried food and taken it back to the *Mayflower*. The Nauset folk thought that was stealing.'

'Well it was, wasn't it?'

'I suppose it was. And reports of that "fight" and the missing food arrived in Plymouth before the Pilgrims did. Things could have been very tricky when they did show up.

'Here's where the luck comes in. Stealing was a big crime for the Wampanoag. But they had other worries. They were at war with their neighbours, the Narragansett. Having the Pilgrims as friends would help them in case of a Narragansett attack.'

• 1620 VOYAGE OF THE MAYFLOWER •

Fletch had been pacing back and forth while his uncle was speaking. Finally he butted in: 'How could they talk to each other? The Pilgrims didn't speak the Wampanoag language. And the Wampanoag didn't speak English!'

'Good question. Which leads me to the real bit of Pilgrim luck. One of the Wampanoag, called Squanto, could speak English. Thomas Hunt, an English explorer, had kidnapped Squanto in 1614. Hunt took Squanto back to Europe. So he had lived in Spain and England for five years and had learned to speak English.

'By 1620 Squanto had made it back to his Patuxet home. Massasoit, the Wampanoag leader, asked Squanto to approach the Pilgrims. He arrived with a small group on 22nd March 1621. Squanto spoke briefly with the Pilgrims and told them that he had come in peace.

'The English said that their King James also wanted peace. Squanto then returned to the woods and came back with

• ADVENTURES IN THE REAL WORLD •

Massasoit. The Pilgrims and the Wampanoag came to an agreement. They agreed to live together in peace. And they would help each other in times of danger or attack.'

Fletch was beaming again. He said, 'That really was lucky for the Pilgrims and the Wampanoag!'

'Well, the Pilgrims wouldn't have said it was luck. They would say that God was rewarding them for their beliefs. Luck or not, things really did improve for them after that meeting. For one thing, spring had come. The weather was improving and they had built more houses. Finally everyone could move off the *Mayflower*.

'Plus - and this is really important - Squanto stayed with them for 20 months. During that time he taught them how to farm and fish in their new home. By the way, the rats on board the *Mayflower* were fine. They adapted to the New World quickly, which, of course, is why you and I are here.

• ADVENTURES IN THE REAL WORLD •

'Of course, humans can be a little dimmer than rats, or maybe they're just stubborn. Squanto saw some of the stuff that the Pilgrims were still eating. Stuff that had crossed the Atlantic. Soggy biscuits, dried meat and fruit with worms crawling inside. He showed them how the shore was full of shellfish. They just had to collect clams, mussels and oysters when the tide went out.

'They could use nets and baskets to catch eels and herring in the river and bay. And any fish that didn't get eaten would get buried. Why? Because it made the soil richer. Then they could grow lots of maize, pumpkins and squash.

'Squanto also showed the Pilgrims how to hunt. Back in England, only the rich were allowed to hunt. The Pilgrims shot deer, ducks and rabbit for food. Squanto helped them trap beaver and other animals for fur - fur that would be valuable back in England. So the Pilgrims could pay back the money they borrowed for the voyage.

• 1620 VOYAGE OF THE MAYFLOWER •

'By the autumn of 1621, the Pilgrims were a lot healthier. They were even able to harvest some of the crops that they'd planted

• ADVENTURES IN THE REAL WORLD •

in the spring. So much so that they planned a harvest festival, just like the ones they knew in England.'

Fletch was licking his lips again. 'Do I feel a Thanksgiving Dinner coming on?'

'Oh, Fletch,' Norman sighed, rolling his eyes.

THE FIRST THANKSGIVING?

Sometime between September and November 1621, the 52 Pilgrims invited 90 of their Wampanoag neighbours to a feast. They didn't call it Thanksgiving. Instead they called it a harvest meal. The main Thanksgiving attraction nowadays is turkey. Some Americans even call Thanksgiving 'Turkey Day'. But turkey might not have been part of that famous meal in 1621. Instead, people had venison (deer meat), pumpkins, maize, cranberries, bread, clams and eels. Some people say that Squanto arrived with his own food – just to make sure he'd have enough to eat!

• 1620 VOYAGE OF THE MAYFLOWER •

• ADVENTURES IN THE REAL WORLD •

EPILOGUE

Norman and Fletch could hear plates being cleared away upstairs. The Thanksgiving feast was coming to an end. Soon the humans would be yawning and drifting off to sleep for a long afternoon nap. Fletch was trying hard not to yawn himself. After all, he'd also been feasting all afternoon and a little shut-eye seemed like a good idea. But he felt there was more to this story yet.

'So, Uncle Norman. We know that the Pilgrims weren't the first English settlers in America. And I've been told that their Thanksgiving wasn't the first over here either. Hadn't some Spanish settlers cooked similar feasts before they did? So what makes the Pilgrims so special?'

• ADVENTURES IN THE REAL WORLD •

'Well, Fletch, you've got a point. But it's still true that most Americans see the Pilgrims as the founders of their country. In a way, it's funny because they weren't all that successful once they got here. Remember how Squanto had to show them how to hunt, because none of them knew how? Well, they never really did get very good at it. Same with fishing.

'Plus, another English colony started up in 1628, just eight years after the *Mayflower* voyage. The Massachusetts Bay Colony was just to the north of Plymouth and it grew up around the city of Boston. Lots more English people sailed across to that colony and it became more successful.'

Fletch was wide awake again. He'd been to Boston once, stowing away on a boat from Plymouth. 'So were the two colonies a bit like rival teams?'

'In a way, except one team kept getting bigger and more successful, and it wasn't the Pilgrims' team. In 1691, the Plymouth Colony merged with the Massachusetts Bay

• 1620 VOYAGE OF THE MAYFLOWER •

Colony. The larger group became known as the Province of Massachusetts Bay.

'So although the *Mayflower* settlement was only "independent" for about 70 years, its memory lives on. That's because unlike other European colonists in North America, the *Mayflower* passengers paved the way for an independent United States of America.

'The *Mayflower Compact*, which the male passengers signed in 1620, did pledge loyalty to the British Crown. But beyond that it said something very important: that the Colony would have the power to make its own laws and to govern itself. And the people living there would respect and obey those laws.

'Exactly 156 years later, representatives of 13 British colonies signed another important document, the Declaration of Independence. It set the stage for the American War of Independence. Many of those who signed it were inspired by the *Mayflower Compact*.'

• ADVENTURES IN THE REAL WORLD •

Norman, now using his 'I'm saying something important' voice, said: 'If those *Mayflower* passengers hadn't created the *Mayflower Compact,* then maybe all of the British colonies would have remained loyal to the British Crown. You'd see the Queen's head on every coin and stamp. Instead of flying the Stars and Stripes, boats out in that harbour would have the Union Jack.'

Fletch piped up to have the last word. 'And we'd be forced to eat Marmite instead of good old American peanut butter!'

• 1620 VOYAGE OF THE MAYFLOWER •

• ADVENTURES IN THE REAL WORLD •

TIMELINE

1533: King Henry VIII cuts ties with the Catholic Church and declares himself head of the Church of England.

1558: Elizabeth I is crowned Queen. She aims to steer the Church of England into a 'middle way' between Catholic and Protestant practices. But laws force all English people - including Catholics and extreme Protestants - to attend Church of England services.

1558 onwards: English Protestants fall mainly into two groups: Puritans (who want to 'purify' the Church of England but remain in it) and Separatists (who call for a completely new Church).

1607: Jamestown, Virginia becomes the first English settlement in North America.

1608: A group of Separatists leave England to find religious freedom in the Netherlands. They settle in the Dutch city of Leiden.

1619: Separatists in England find people to sponsor their voyage and the deal includes hiring the cargo ship the *Mayflower* and its crew.

• 1620 VOYAGE OF THE MAYFLOWER •

1620, 22nd July: Separatists in Leiden sail from the Dutch port of Delfshaven on board the *Speedwell*. They aim to meet other Separatists at the English port of Southampton.

5th August: The *Speedwell* and *Mayflower* leave Southampton, bound for North America.

12th August: The two ships return to the English port of Dartmouth after the *Speedwell* develops leaks.

21st August: The two ships leave England again, but once more have to come back because of leaks on the *Speedwell*. They return to the English port of Plymouth and decide to set out again on just one ship, the *Mayflower*.

6th September: Some Separatists decide to remain in England or Leiden. The rest (now remembered as 'Pilgrims') set sail on the *Mayflower*.

9th November: Sailors on the *Mayflower* spot land. It is the tip of Cape Cod in what is now the state of Massachusetts. The captain decides to continue to its original destination, 200 miles further south.

11th November: Rough seas and bad weather force the *Mayflower* to turn back. It anchors in a sheltered harbour near the tip of Cape Cod.

• ADVENTURES IN THE REAL WORLD •

11th November: The adult male passengers of the *Mayflower* sign the *Mayflower Compact*. It expresses their loyalty to the English King. But it also states that the settlers will govern themselves and make and obey their own laws.

11th November: John Carver, the first person to sign the *Mayflower Compact*, is chosen to be governor of the settlement.

13th November: The Pilgrims first set foot on land.

16th November: The Pilgrims decide to leave Cape Cod and sail across Massachusetts Bay to settle on the mainland.

25th December: Work begins on the first new building in the settlement of Plymouth.

• 1620 VOYAGE OF THE MAYFLOWER •

GLOSSARY

Aft: Near, towards or at the rear of a ship.

Ancestor: A person from the past who is related to someone many years later.

Armada: A large fleet of naval ships.

Becalmed: (Of a sailing ship or boat) drifting at sea because there is no wind to fill the sails.

Cape Cod: A curving peninsula that extends 113 km east from the Massachusetts mainland into the Atlantic Ocean.

Colony: A place where people settle although they remain loyal to their home country.

Crew: The sailors and other people who work on a ship.

Deck: A level part of a ship, like a floor in a building.

• ADVENTURES IN THE REAL WORLD •

Declaration of Independence: A document signed by members of 13 British North American colonies in 1776. It announced that those 13 colonies considered themselves independent and no longer under British rule.

Descendant: A person who comes from a given ancestor or ancestors.

Execute: To kill because a law has been broken.

Firebox: A type of basic stove on old ships. It was simply a metal box resting on beams and filled with sand. Cooking fires would be lit on the sand.

Flex: To bend and straighten (often an arm or a leg) again and again.

Fore: Near, towards or at the front of a ship.

Forefather: An ancestor, especially one who lived in the same place as a descendant nowadays.

Governor: A person chosen or elected to rule (govern) a particular place, like a colony.

Hoist: To raise something (like a sail or a flag), usually using ropes to help pull it up.

• 1620 VOYAGE OF THE MAYFLOWER •

Investor: Someone who lets his or her money be used by other people, expecting that those other people will pay back more than they received.

Mainland: A larger area of land near an island or peninsula.

Pilgrim: A person who goes to a holy place or who is on a religious journey. The word also describes the English Separatists who travelled to North America on the *Mayflower*.

Pope: The elected leader of the Catholic Church.

Protestant: A Christian Church, or member of that Church, that rejects many of the practices and some of the beliefs of the Catholic Church.

Puritan: A member of the Church of England with strong Protestant beliefs but who chose to remain within that Church rather than split away.

Separatist: An English Protestant in the 1500s and 1600s who wanted to separate from the Church of England rather than try to change it from within.

Wampanoag: A Native American nation living in eastern Massachusetts, where the Pilgrims landed.

INDEX

A
Atlantic ocean 4, 33, 40, 45–46, 53–54, 67, 75, 108, 123

B
Boleyn, Anne 17, 19, 21
Boston 114
Bradford, William 54, 77, 94
Brewster, William 28, 50, 71

C
Cape Cod 4, 73–75, 81, 84, 88, 101, 121–123
Carver, John 71, 94, 122
Church of England 17–22, 27, 29, 34, 38, 43, 58, 120, 125

D
Declaration of Independence 79, 115, 124
Delfshaven 121

E
Elizabeth I, Queen 20–22, 26, 33–34, 120

F
First Encounter Beach 81
Forefathers Day 87–88

H
Henry VIII, King 16–20, 26, 120
Hudson river 58, 73–74
Hunt, Thomas 103

J
James I, King 26–27, 33, 103
Jamestown 33, 58, 73, 120

L
Leiden 36–37, 45, 47, 49, 120–121

M

maize 92, 105, 108, 110
Mary, Queen 17, 20–21
Massasoit 103–104
Mayflower Compact 77, 79, 94, 115–116, 122

N

Narragansett 102

P

Patuxet 90–91, 97, 103
Plymouth, Massachusetts 8–9, 37–38, 53, 83–84, 87–89, 96–97, 102, 114, 122
Pope 16–18, 125
Protestants 15–16, 18–22, 27, 35–36, 120, 125
Puritans 22, 120, 125

S

Scrooby 22, 28
seaweed 106–107
Separatists 21–22, 27–29, 32–36, 38, 40, 45–51, 55–56, 71, 120–121, 125
Southampton 48, 51, 121
Spanish Armada 19

Speedwell 45, 47, 51–53, 121
Squanto 103–104, 108, 110, 114
Standish, Myles 81–82, 101–102

T

Thanksgiving 8, 37, 87, 110, 113
turkey 9, 110

V

Virginia 33–34, 38, 58, 73, 76–77, 79, 84, 89, 92, 120

W

Wampanoag 9, 90, 97, 101–104, 110, 125
wigwams 90

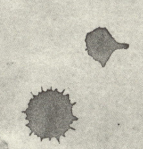

• ADVENTURES IN THE REAL WORLD •